I0821938

STRONG, HEALTHY GIRLS

BEING A LEADER

By Anne E. Johnson

CONTENT CONSULTANT

Dr. Amanda J. Rose
Professor of Psychological Sciences
University of Missouri

An Imprint of Abdo Publishing | abdobooks.com

abdobooks.com

Published by Abdo Publishing, a division of ABDO, PO Box 398166, Minneapolis, Minnesota 55439.

Printed in the United States of America, North Mankato, Minnesota.
082020
012021

Cover Photo: Jihan Nafiaa Zahri/Shutterstock Images
Interior Photos: Shutterstock Images, 8, 23, 30, 42, 95; Pixel-Shot/Shutterstock Images, 11; Photographee/Shutterstock Images, 13; iStockphoto, 14, 18, 20, 25, 35, 50, 60, 82, 90, 93; Monkey Business Images/iStockphoto, 27; Rawpixel/iStockphoto, 33, 37; Aleksandr Markin/Shutterstock Images, 45; Susan Leggett/Shutterstock Images, 47; SDI Productions/iStockphoto, 54, 81, 86–87; Mesha Photo/iStockphoto, 57; Michael Jung/Shutterstock Images, 62; Motortion Films/Shutterstock Images, 66; Air Images/Shutterstock Images, 70; Wave Break Media/Shutterstock Images, 72–73; Look Studio/Shutterstock Images, 78; Jonas Petrovas/Shutterstock Images, 98–99

Editor: Megan Ellis
Series Designer: Nikki Nordby

Library of Congress Control Number: 2019954421
Publisher's Cataloging-in-Publication Data

Names: Johnson, Anne E., author.
Title: Being a leader / by Anne E. Johnson
Description: Minneapolis, Minnesota : Abdo Publishing, 2021 | Series: Strong, healthy girls | Includes online resources and index.
Identifiers: ISBN 9781532192135 (lib. bdg.) | ISBN 9781098210038 (ebook)
Subjects: LCSH: Leadership in adolescents--Juvenile literature. | Girls' leadership--Juvenile literature. | Attitude (Psychology)--Juvenile literature. | Assertiveness (Psychology)--Juvenile literature. | Interpersonal relations--Juvenile literature. | Self-confidence in adolescence--Juvenile literature.
Classification: DDC 155.533--dc23

CONTENTS

DR. AMANDA

Dr. Amanda J. Rose has always been interested in relationships. Our closest relationships can bring us incredible happiness, but when our relationships don't go well, life can be very hard. Different relationships are important at different stages of life, with friendships being especially important for adolescents. Dr. Rose has been studying girls' friendships for more than 20 years, with more than 5,000 youth participating in her research projects.

Dr. Rose grew up in Ohio and attended college at Ohio State University, where she majored in psychology and minored in English. Her senior thesis was her first research project on adolescence. After graduating summa cum laude, Dr. Rose went on to study developmental psychology at the University of Illinois at Urbana–Champaign. There she earned her master's degree and her doctorate. For her master's thesis and doctoral dissertation, she studied how girls and boys handle conflict in their friendships and how they support each other in times of stress.

In 1999, Dr. Rose joined the faculty at the University of Missouri as a founding member of the Developmental Psychology Training Program in the Department of Psychological Sciences. Together with her students, she has conducted many research studies, with a focus on the benefits and challenges of girls' friendships. This research has been funded by the National Institute of Mental Health. During her time at the University of Missouri, Dr. Rose has received many honors and awards, including an Early Scientific Achievement Award from the Society for Research in Child Development and a Kemper Fellowship for Excellence in Teaching, one of the highest teaching honors awarded at the University of Missouri.

Dr. Rose lives in Columbia, Missouri, with her husband, her teenaged daughter and son, and her yellow Labrador retriever, Charlie.

TAKE IT FROM ME

When I was in high school, I was very into making art. The school's art teacher encouraged me to try different mediums such as watercolor, acrylic, and clay. I asked my study hall teacher if I could occasionally get a hall pass so that I could work on my projects in the art room during that time. My study hall teacher said that he couldn't give me a pass because he didn't believe that art counted as studying. This struck me as completely unfair. Art was a class, so *somebody* must think art was a subject you could study!

I gathered a group of arts students and teachers who felt the same way. Together, we signed a letter that said art and music should be considered eligible for study hall passes. The principal was impressed by our dedication, and the change to allow hall passes for arts classes went into effect.

You don't have to be class president, let alone president of the United States, to make a difference as a leader. Good leaders often approach conflicts from a place of wanting to understand, rather than coming in with assumptions about the situation.

Without a clear understanding, a leader may not be effective. By honing your listening skills and developing empathy, you can understand the emotional reactions of others.

While it's tempting to make big promises, that approach typically doesn't turn out well if you can't follow through with them. The relationship between leader and followers breaks down if the vision isn't realistic. A similar situation occurs when a leader tries to make people change the habits they're used to without clearly explaining exactly what she has in mind or why it's worth the effort to change.

You can take the lead in your school or community. You might lead a sports team, inspiring your players to give their all and helping to work out conflict within the team, or you might lead others to make better choices and treat their peers with kindness. If you're interested in being a leader, there is always a place for you to exercise your leadership skills.

YOUR FRIEND,
ANNE

CHAPTER ONE

THE SHY LEADER

When people hear the word *leader*, they may picture someone who has a particular set of traits. They may assume all leaders are strong and fearless, or that leadership requires a powerful, loud voice. Commonly, they'll imagine a crowd listening to that leader and doing whatever he or she tells them. Other people may believe that leaders can only be men or members of certain races or religions.

However, there are several problems with these ideas about who can and can't be leaders. Some people might be unwilling to follow someone who would make a great leader just because that person doesn't look or sound like what they expect. Groups, businesses, and even governments sometimes end up with a poor leader because they chose someone based solely on their expectations of what a leader should be.

Someone who is shy may not think she has the qualities to be a good leader. But often, it may just mean that the person has convinced herself that shyness is a negative quality for a leader. A change in perspective can help someone on the road to leadership. Often, finding the right project to hone your leadership skills will give you the confidence to try leading.

MIA'S STORY

Mia and the other teens in her youth group were gathered in the church basement for their weekly meeting. Pastor Jack pointed at them. "I just know that one of you is the perfect person to represent us at the Youth Leadership Conference in Springfield next month. It's a big honor for whoever gets to go." He held up a clipboard. "On your way out the door, sign your name on this piece of paper if you're interested. Next week, we'll take a vote."

Mia's mind raced, wondering what she would do at the camp if she were to sign that paper. Although she didn't know how to express it in words, she felt like she had the potential to make a difference if she had the opportunity to be a leader. But then she noticed that everyone was looking at Greg. Greg was the captain of the high school lacrosse team, which he'd led to a division championship last year. He had a way of charming people, and he didn't ever seem to be worried or afraid. It was easy to imagine him leading their group at the conference.

Mia and her friend Rebecca watched Greg sign the clipboard. "He's a born leader," said Mia, trying to shake off a feeling of disappointment.

Rebecca agreed. But then she added, “You should sign up too, Mia.”

Mia was surprised. “Me? I am not a leader. I feel like I’m going to hurl just getting called on in class,” she said. “And that’s when I know the answer!”

“Me? I am not a leader. I feel like I’m going to hurl just getting called on in class.”

“You’re the most organized person I know,” Rebecca said. “When we had that Spanish club fundraiser, you somehow managed to keep track of exactly who had promised to give how much. I would have completely screwed that up.”

Before Mia could protest, Rebecca went on. "Not to mention that you're just such a good person. You care about everybody. What better quality could you possibly have? Being a leader is all about caring, and you're the most caring person I know."

"Being a leader is all about caring, and you're the most caring person I know."

"That's sweet, but forget it," said Mia. She could feel herself blushing at all of the praise. "Shy people can't be leaders." But in the back of her mind, she thought that Rebecca had made a lot of sense. However, she didn't have the nerve to sign up, so she left the room without looking at the paper.

TALK ABOUT IT

- **Do you see yourself as a leader? Why or why not?**
- **What do you think it would take to represent a group you're part of?**

***

When the youth group voted the following week, Greg easily won the vote. Just as Mia suspected, everyone assumed Greg was the perfect leader to represent them. But as she glanced at his famous grin, she wondered whether she could have done the job just as well. It made her a little sad that she wouldn't find out, but it also felt inevitable. She truly believed she wasn't leader material.

The next day, Rebecca invited Mia to come over after school. "No thanks," said Mia. "I'm going to volunteer at the animal rescue center for a couple of hours. Want to come with?"

"Sure, why not," Rebecca said. "It might be fun."

While riding their bikes to the rescue center, they ran into some boys from their youth group. One of them was Greg.

"Congrats on the leaders' conference," Rebecca said.

"Thanks," said Greg. "Where are you two heading?"

"To volunteer at the animal rescue," said Mia. "After we clean up the cages, we can play with the puppies. Want to join us?"

Greg snorted when he laughed. "No way. Why would I go work somewhere when I have the afternoon off?" One of his friends laughed too. But the third boy, Nathan, stepped toward Mia shyly.

"I'd love to play with the puppies," he said.

"Come on, Nathan," said Greg. "Don't be pathetic."

Mia stepped angrily between Nathan and Greg. "There is nothing pathetic about liking something. What if he said that about your trip to the youth leadership conference?"

Greg rolled his eyes. "Everyone knows that trip is stupid. I just want three nights away from my parents so I can play video games without them getting on my case."

Regretting now that she hadn't put herself up for the vote, Mia sighed. She said quietly to Nathan, "It would be really great if you came with us. Will you?"

TALK ABOUT IT

- **Why did people think Greg would be a good leader? How does he show whether or not he would be?**
- **What does it tell you when a leader doesn't want to get involved in a project with his or her followers?**

Nathan nodded and picked up his bike so they could walk at the same pace to the rescue center. The volunteer on duty, Mrs. Evans, was excited to see them. "Three volunteers at once. That's fantastic! Thanks so much for coming to help."

"It was Mia's idea," said Rebecca. "She talked us both into it. She really cares about those puppies!"

Mrs. Evans shook Mia's hand. "You have the makings of an excellent leader, Mia."

Mia was surprised. She'd thought that her shyness meant that she couldn't be a leader at all. But Mrs. Evans had a point. Greg seemed like a good leader, but deep down he wasn't doing it for the right reasons. Mia resolved to not let her shyness hold her back from believing in herself. She just needed to be a leader in her own way—one that included a lot of puppy kisses!

TALK ABOUT IT

- **What is it about Mia's actions that make her a leader?**
- **What are some things you can do to lead by example?**

ASK THE EXPERT

When Mia thought of leading as an abstract thing, it didn't seem like something she could do. But when helping animals, something she was passionate about, she became a leader without even trying. Greg, on the other hand, showed that he wasn't willing to be a great leader. Greg didn't want to lead for the benefit of his group—he just wanted more time to play video games. He was thinking about his own needs instead of feeling driven to make positive changes for the group.

The world is full of people who sound good but aren't good or effective leaders. Recognizing these people for what they are can be tricky, but it's essential if you want to protect society against bad leaders. Their charisma blinds us, and we don't notice that they have nothing positive to offer. It's a good habit to try to see beneath the surface of someone before you decide to trust them.

Leadership is needed in many aspects of life. Leadership isn't always a big, glamorous thing. It can happen in small, quiet ways. Participating in volunteer work is a great way to gain leadership skills. You may even gain the confidence to jump into more prominent leadership positions later. Just because you don't lead a particular group doesn't mean you'll never be a leader. Keep your eyes open for chances to lead in whatever way suits your unique personality.

GET HEALTHY

- Get involved in a cause or activity you're passionate about. Try volunteering somewhere to make the world a better place.
- Write a list of things you care most about and brainstorm ideas about what you can do to support or improve those things.
- Write a pretend news article that describes some specific thing you, and only you, were able to do to make your group, school, or community a better place.
- Everyone has the potential to be a leader. Keep challenging yourself and develop at your own pace.

THE LAST WORD FROM ANNE

There are many people out there who can be inspiring leaders if you give them a chance. One year at the school where I teach, the students voted on which student to send as the school's representative to a music conference. He was introverted and shy, but the other students took the time to listen closely to him when he talked about why he wanted to go to that conference. They were impressed by his ambition and his willingness to improve music education in the United States. He wasn't most people's idea of a leader, but the students were confident that he had their best interests at heart.

Don't worry that you don't fit into a preconceived mold of what a leader "should" be like. There's a place for you at the front once you figure out your strengths. You may have to wait until the right opportunity presents itself.

CHAPTER TWO

LEARNING TO LISTEN

While leaders often have the best intentions to keep their group running smoothly without stress or worry, there's no way to avoid conflict entirely. Sometimes a good leader has to help group members and peers move past the conflict so they can work together.

An important skill for working through conflicts is active listening, which might be described as listening with your heart and mind, not just your ears. When you listen actively, you get a better understanding of what is being said, so that you'll not only hear the words, but *why* and *how* the person said them.

It's tempting to let yourself become frustrated with group members who can't seem to get along. But by using active listening, you may be able to reassure group members that their feelings are valued. You can also try to remove yourself from the equation and understand the situation from another person's point of view. That means letting others explain their perspective while you listen attentively rather than talk about your own feelings. Wei learned how to be a better leader when she needed to help with a conflict in on her soccer team.

WEI'S STORY

The Milton High School girls' soccer team was usually the best in their region, but lately they hadn't been playing up to their usual standards. They couldn't get the ball across the field like they used to or even defend their own goal. The team's energy seemed to have evaporated.

As team captain, Wei wanted to help get the girls fired up again, but her strategies didn't seem to be working. Her cheers fell flat, and her teammates didn't accept her congratulatory hugs. When she hollered, "You can do it!" at her teammates during a game, another player quipped, "Or not!" This caused several of the other girls to laugh. Wei got the sense that the team had just given up.

After the game, which they'd lost by three points, Wei kept her eyes and ears open in the locker room hoping to get to the bottom of what was happening with the rest of the team. It didn't take long before she figured out what was missing. There was almost no talking at all, which was definitely not normal behavior in a locker room. At first Wei wondered if the glum silence was due to low morale because of the game loss. She looked around the locker room for any signs of a bigger problem. Then Wei noticed something odd.

On her way to the showers, Marie, the team's goalie, passed her friend Leanne. Normally they talked and joked together constantly, but as Wei watched, they both looked away from each other as if they were strangers. Marie high-fived a couple of other girls, who sneered at Leanne. Some other players shifted uncomfortably, their eyes on the floor.

When Marie left the locker room, Wei followed her out into the parking lot so they could chat in private. "Hey," said Wei.

"What?" Marie snapped. She wiped her eyes. Her cheeks were wet. She'd been crying. "Don't sneak up on me."

"Sorry," said Wei. She held up her hands. "I just wondered what was wrong between you and Leanne."

Marie took a sharp breath. Her shoulders tensed and she crossed her arms. "It's not your problem. Leave me alone."

"I'm just trying to help," Wei tried to assure her. "You two usually get along so well, but I've been noticing that you seem angry with each other."

Marie practically growled out her reply. "I told you to leave me alone. What's going on between Leanne and me is between Leanne and me. Is that so hard to understand?"

That evasive answer just made Wei frustrated. Wei thought that maybe if she could push Marie harder, she

TALK ABOUT IT

- **Have you ever seen a situation where someone's bad mood brought everyone else down? What, if anything, did you do about it?**
- **Was there ever a time when your own disagreement with a friend affected school or extracurricular activities? How did you handle the situation?**

could get some answers. "You just admitted to me there's something wrong, and it's affecting the whole team," Wei said angrily. "Everybody's feeling the stress between you two. Maybe if you'd just talk about it, our teammates could relax and focus on their playing."

"Maybe if you'd just talk about it, our teammates could relax and focus on their playing."

"Oh, so I'm making the team lose now?" Marie said. "Well, maybe you should tell Coach to kick me off the team then!" Marie turned and ran away down the sidewalk, leaving Wei even more confused.

TALK ABOUT IT

- **Why is Marie so hostile to Wei?**
- **What could Wei have done differently to put Marie at ease?**

Wei lay awake that night thinking about why Marie had been so upset. *I was ready to listen to her*, Wei told herself, baffled by what had gone wrong. However, when Wei thought about it more, she realized that she'd reacted in anger to Marie instead of really listening. No wonder Marie got so upset!

***

At school the next day, Wei found Leanne in a corner of the cafeteria, as far away across the room from Marie as possible. It occurred to Wei that this might be a chance for a redo, or at least an approach from the other direction by seeing what Leanne had to say. Promising herself not to force Leanne to talk about things that made her uncomfortable, Wei started with a neutral topic. "We did a little better in the game yesterday than we have been," Wei said as she slid her tray next to Leanne's.

Leanne shrugged. "I guess."

"You sound kind of bummed," said Wei, picking her words carefully. "Is it about the team?"

Leanne stabbed her fork into a pile of corn kernels. "I guess."

Wei was determined to be more sensitive and empathetic than she had been with Marie. She said, "Did somebody upset you?"

Slamming down her fork, Leanne blurted out, "Marie did! You should kick her off the team!"

"Oh! Um," Wei said. She tried to sound calm, but she needed more information. "Why do you say that?"

"She keeps missing the ball. She's the goalie." As she spoke, Leanne kept her eyes down and tore her napkin in pieces. "A goalie should be able to keep the ball out of the goal. She's *stupid*."

Wei thought about Marie's performance. It wasn't any worse than anyone else's. And before the last few games, Marie had saved almost every goal that came her way. Wei figured that this

fight between Leanne and Marie might not actually have anything to do with soccer at all.

She took a breath and tried again. "I never see you and Marie together anymore," Wei said, taking a bite of her food.

Leanne said, "She thinks she's too good for me now that she sits with the other kids who made Homecoming Court." She pointed across the lunchroom. Marie was sitting at a table with a few other people.

"Did Marie tell you she doesn't like you anymore?" Wei asked Leanne, who shook her head. "Then she's probably still your friend! Why don't you two talk to each other and see what's going on?"

Leanne sighed. "I hadn't thought about it like that," she said.

The next time Marie looked over, Leanne gave her a small wave. Marie looked surprised, but after a few seconds she nodded slightly, even flashing a shy smile.

TALK ABOUT IT

- **What choices did Wei make that kept Leanne talking?**
- **What clues is Leanne giving about how she really feels?**

"Why don't you two talk to each other and see what's going on?"

"Looks to me like your friendship isn't necessarily over," said Wei. "Maybe you should text her and see if you guys can work it out." As Leanne got out her phone, Wei left the table, her spirits lifted by a hope that the mood in the locker room was about to improve. Maybe they would even start winning games again!

TALK ABOUT IT

- **Have you ever helped someone through a problem by listening to them? How did you show you were listening? What did the other person do?**
- **What are some things to watch and listen for that can help you figure out what a person really means?**

ASK THE EXPERT

Given how powerful emotions can be, they have the potential to affect both individuals and groups. Part of a leader's job is to figure out what emotional tensions are causing stress within the group. Getting the context for why people behave the way they do is key to leading a group out of conflict.

When Wei first noticed the tension between Marie and Leanne, her intentions were good. But pushing someone for information isn't the same as giving them an opportunity to tell you their perspective on what's happening. Wei approached Marie full of assumptions, which caused Marie to feel attacked, so she shut down and walked away. When Wei started a conversation with Leanne, she took a different approach. Wei's active listening allowed Leanne to feel safe about expressing herself.

One technique that promotes active listening is observation. You can gather a lot of information from what you see. Body language sometimes speaks louder than words. When Marie crossed her arms, it was a sign of distrust and anger. Leanne's refusal to look Wei in the eye indicated that she wanted to avoid talking about the true issue. The way she spoke also gave Wei a clue that she was clearly frustrated about something else. When you listen actively, you can often hear more than you would otherwise, reaching a better understanding of the situation.

GET HEALTHY

- Imagine a person has suddenly started acting mean to everyone. Make a list of ten things that might be going on in someone's life to change that person's personality.
- Next time you're in the lunchroom or other crowded place, watch people across the room talking to each other. What can you tell just from their posture, facial expressions, hand motions, and other body language?
- Practice using language that shows others you're listening to them. When you're speaking to someone who wants you to understand their position, try responding with these phrases: "I see what you're saying." "That must have been upsetting/scary/amazing." "That relates to what [another person] was saying before."

THE LAST WORD FROM ANNE

A successful team feels comfortable talking to its leader when things go wrong, and it's the leader's responsibility to learn the skills needed to listen in a meaningful way.

It's to everyone's advantage if the tensions in a group can be kept as low as possible, and a leader has the potential to make a big difference in that regard. As Wei found out, reaching out to individual members of the group who are struggling can be a powerful tool for rebuilding the harmony in a group.

Active listening is a gift you give others. It makes them feel important and understood while also demonstrating that they're an essential part of the group. You are proving that their thoughts and actions matter.

CHAPTER THREE

PROBLEMS WITH NEW IDEAS

People are creatures of habit. They tend to do things the same way over and over. Change takes a lot of effort, and it can be frightening. There's no way to be certain whether a new way of doing things will actually be better than the old way. Because of this, it often feels easier to allow things to remain as they are.

This resistance to change can be particularly strong in groups. When someone comes in who wants to shake things up, that person will often face a lot of resistance. This may be because group members are used to the way things have always been. Feeling forced by a leader to learn new things can bring about resentment and stress if the group members don't understand what they're supposed to do. They also might think that everything is fine just the way it is.

Ironically, this kind of resistance is often strongest when change is most needed. Sometimes the old way of doing things has stopped working. Members of a failing group tend to dig in their heels. This problem tends to occur when the leader's vision isn't clearly expressed. It's the leader's responsibility to convince the group that her new plan is a good one and to assure everybody that they will have a role to play.

KRISTIN'S STORY

Because she was a freshman, Kristin had never been to the homecoming dance before. Freshmen didn't usually join homecoming committee. But Kristin's older sister Brianna, who attended some committee meetings last year, told her that the committee's job was primarily decorating the gym for the dance after the football game.

Considering that there was nothing Kristin loved more than decorating for a party, she decided to attend the meeting. That Thursday afternoon, she was surprised when only six other kids showed up. They nodded at her and muttered, "Hi," which didn't exactly make her feel welcome.

A boy named Jasper seemed to be in charge. "We'll get green tablecloths and matching cups, of course," he said, glancing at a list. "We can make that green punch recipe from last year. It

tasted kind of weird, but it matches the tablecloth, so it works. Principal Vasquez says the usual DJ can do the music for the dance. Anything else I'm forgetting?"

Nobody said anything. One girl yawned, while three of the others were glued to their phones. Kristin was nervous to speak up, but she couldn't sit silently while the party continued being planned so poorly!

Kristin said, "This sounds kind of boring. Shouldn't it be fun?"

"This sounds kind of boring. Shouldn't it be fun?"

Now everyone was looking at her, so she thought fast. "My cousin Alexandra has an amazing band. I mean, *amazing*. They're always looking for places to play, so I bet they'd play for cheaper than some boring old DJ."

"Mr. Bellini is a nice old guy," said an older girl. "He works at my dad's office."

"OK," said Kristin, "but does he play the best music? Does he get the crowd excited?"

"He's fine," said a boy who was playing a game on his phone. "He's who we always get."

Kristin's blood pumped fast, and she couldn't stop herself. "You guys, this homecoming could be the best ever! I mean, we could find volunteers to make some green and white table decorations, so the gym will look classy in the school colors. And there's lots of great recipes for punch. There's absolutely no reason for the punch to taste weird."

She stood up and continued talking. "Let's get some white crepe paper to hang from the green tablecloths. I pinned some ideas on Pinterest that you can check out—there's a DIY to make a walkway out of plywood and paper flowers. Wouldn't that be nice? It won't even cost more money to make this party great if we can figure out better ways to spend the money."

TALK ABOUT IT

- **Is the Homecoming Committee group what Kristin expected? Why or why not?**
- **Do you think Jasper is a good leader? What could he do differently to welcome Kristin into the group?**

There was an awkward silence for a few seconds, until Jasper said, "What's your *problem*, anyway?"

Kristin gasped. "My problem?"

"Yeah," Jasper said, scowling. "This is your first meeting and you're acting like you want to take over? No way. Our decorations have never been a problem, so there's no reason to change anything now."

Kristin felt incredibly embarrassed and sat down silently, a sick feeling in her stomach. As the students

TALK ABOUT IT

- **What are some things Kristin could have done differently to present her ideas?**
- **Was she acting like a leader when she discussed her ideas with the group? Why or why not?**

around her continued planning, Kristin became more determined to make some positive changes.

***

That evening, she asked Brianna, "Do you know any of the kids on this year's committee?"

"Nylah is on it, I'm pretty sure," Brianna said. "She's a junior, kind of tall, and wears a hijab."

"OK, I think I remember who she was," Kristin said. "Do you know how she feels about the committee?"

"I know she's frustrated with Jasper's leadership," Brianna said, "but other than that, I don't know anything else. Sorry, sis."

A flicker of hope lifted Kristin's mood, and a plan formed in her mind.

***

The next day, Kristin found Nylah at her locker and didn't waste any time getting to the point. "I'm sorry if I was rude in the committee meeting," Kristin said. "I got so excited about making this dance the best one yet!"

Nylah smiled, looking much friendlier than she had yesterday. "I totally understand,

TALK ABOUT IT

- **Why do you think the other students had such a bad reaction to what Kristin said? How would you have felt in their shoes?**
- **What other questions could Kristin have asked her sister?**

but you'd better save that excitement. We just do the same thing every year."

Kristin knew she had to be careful, so she gently asked, "But do we have to? I mean, it sounds like the punch doesn't even taste good!"

"It's awful," Nylah said, "but Jasper insists on doing it the easy way, and he hates having to do more work."

"I totally understand, but you'd better save that excitement."

As Nylah walked off to class, Kristin began planning how she'd approach the next committee meeting. She wrote down a few ideas in a composition notebook so she'd be prepared to speak next time. And she made sure that the changes were ones the group could get behind too. If nobody liked the punch, it might be easiest to start there. At least, Kristin hoped.

She still had knots in her stomach at the idea of speaking up in the group again, especially in front of Jasper. But Kristin flipped to the next page in her notebook and tried to list some reasons why Jasper might have been so upset during the last meeting. Kristin had *maybe* gone a bit overboard with her suggestions. She'd wanted to change everything on the first day. No wonder Jasper had gotten mad. Kristin would need the next week to plan how to approach the group at their upcoming meeting.

***

When the meeting rolled around, Jasper seemed surprised that Kristin came back. The meeting had barely been called to order before Kristin raised her hand to speak.

"I know I maybe didn't get off on the right foot," she said quickly. The other committee members chuckled. "And for that, I'm sorry. But I think there are a couple little things we can change about the dance that will make it more fun for everyone."

TALK ABOUT IT

- **Why do you think it was important for Kristin to speak to Nylah?**
- **What do you think Kristin learned about group behavior when she asked again about changing the punch?**

With that, Kristin pulled a thermos out of her backpack along with a few cups she'd brought from home. Nylah looked confused, but nodded encouragement at Kristin anyway. Kristin poured five cups of fruit punch she'd made that morning before school. "Try it!" she said. "It's super quick to make. I did it all this morning."

"Really?" Jasper asked, frowning. "I don't believe that."

"Really," Kristin insisted.

Nylah was the first one to pick up a cup. She stared at the green punch suspiciously, but took a sip. Her eyes lit up. "Oh, this is good! Is that pineapple?"

"Pineapple *and* mango," Kristin replied.

The other committee members picked up their own cups. All of them had similar reactions as Nylah. Only Jasper was holding out, but seeing everyone else enjoy the punch, he took a sip himself.

"OK, that's good," Jasper admitted, still frowning. "Definitely better than the other punch."

"So can we make this punch instead?" Kristin asked. "I'll make it ahead of time. That way other committee members can do the things they're interested in too!"

Jasper sighed. "OK, we can make your punch."

Kristin beamed. It may have only been a small victory, but even getting the group to agree on a new punch felt like the first step in becoming a better leader.

ASK THE EXPERT

While creative thinking is an essential aspect of leadership, there's more to being a successful leader than having an idea. Just because you can see all the details clearly in your head doesn't mean you've conveyed them to others in the group. You can't expect support from people who don't understand what you have in mind. Kristin thought she was showing enthusiasm and attentiveness by speaking up about her ideas. However, she didn't consider how all of her new ideas would be received, nor did she have the courtesy to speak respectfully to the group and its current leader. Instead, she came across as rude and disrespectful.

What she did next turned out to be what was best both for her and the group. First, she acknowledged that she wasn't the leader and that she had behaved inappropriately. And then she approached a member to ask for their honest feedback on the situation, so she could better understand the dynamics of the group. With continued respectful behavior and a clear explanation of her ideas, like bringing in a sample of the fruit punch, Kristin might well have been on her way to becoming leader of that committee. If nothing else, she was gaining great experience for leading another committee in the future.

GET HEALTHY

- Think of something in your school or community you wish you could change. Find a few other people who are also interested and brainstorm what could be done to make that change happen.
- Practice how you would suggest a change to someone without making them feel insulted or attacked.
- Write a list of five clubs or activities you would like to get involved in. Then think of ways that you could be a good leader in those clubs or activities.

THE LAST WORD FROM ANNE

Getting your ideas across requires patience and good communication skills. If you can convince people that your idea is not just great, but doable, you're off to an excellent start. If the group can't be made to understand why it's worth the risk to try something new, the members are likely to be more resistant to your idea.

In high school, I had to learn that it wasn't always my place to say how things should be done, and I lost a couple of friends in the process because they felt I wasn't taking them seriously. I've also made the mistake of not acknowledging existing leaders in a group. On the other hand, even when you're not officially the leader, there are appropriate ways and times when you can influence the group's direction. Persuading people to consider what you have to say usually comes down to speaking with respect and communicating your idea clearly. That's when the real conversation can begin.

CHAPTER FOUR

IT'S NOT ABOUT YOU

Leaders sometime face the challenge of not being appreciated for the work they do or for the times they make sacrifices to help the group reach its goal. People have a tendency to complain instead of act, and they often take their frustrations out on their leaders, whether the blame is justified or not. In a situation like that, it's up to the leader to keep a cool head and not overreact to criticism.

No matter how unfair it seems, make sure to consider everyone's point of view. It's possible that the people you're leading aren't getting what they need or want from the group. A good leader will consider their complaints as legitimate, assuming the group members are raising real issues even if their tone or presentation is not constructive. Maybe there's more you could do to understand their suggestions for improvements. Making yourself accessible to criticism and complaints requires humility on your part.

When you're at the head of a group, other members may feel like you have too much power. This may cause them to resent you or even lash out. It may be tough to lead effectively when your feelings are hurt. Leadership takes a lot of discipline, but most of all, you need to be humble and acknowledge that the needs of group members are as important as your own. For some leaders, that's the hardest part.

LEILANI'S STORY

Sound carries easily in an indoor swimming pool. Leilani could hear her teammates talking about her even though she was several lanes away preparing to practice her backstroke for the upcoming meet. "She's so full of herself," Izzy said to one of their teammates.

Coach Keahi had just made Leilani captain of the team. Although Leilani should have been happy, she was distressed to hear her teammates complain about her leadership.

"She's not even that great of a swimmer," Marisol added. "She's only the captain because she won at the last meet."

"She's only the captain because she won at the last meet."

TALK ABOUT IT

- **From Leilani's point of view, why is everyone angry at her?**
- **How could Leilani approach her teammates about their feelings?**

Leilani saw her teammates shoot each other glances when she got out of the pool, her stomach sinking like a rock. She didn't think she could swim with how poorly she felt. She'd just have to fit in an extra workout tomorrow.

At the end of practice, their coach called everyone over to discuss a new rule she was trying out for the next meet. "To keep things fair, everyone will have to earn a slot at the meet during practice the week before," Coach Keahi said. She glanced down at her clipboard. "Except the captain, of course. Leilani gets a spot to lead us to victory!"

At that, several people snorted and even rolled their eyes at the coach, who didn't seem bothered by their attitude. Leilani was angry—not only that they'd been disrespectful to the coach, but also because she didn't deserve to be gossiped about! Leilani was sure that if they were talking behind her back at the pool, they were doing it other places too.

***

That weekend, Coach Keahi drove everyone to the meet at Prospect High in a school van. While no one said anything to Leilani directly, all of the seats next to other people were full by the time she got on the bus. Some people were even saving seats for their friends, using their backpacks to block the extra spots. Leilani had to go to a seat by herself behind everyone else. Instead of singing and laughing with the others during the drive, she stewed over how her teammates were treating her. By the time they reached the meet, she'd decided to quit the team the next day.

By the time they reached the meet, she'd decided to quit the team the next day.

TALK ABOUT IT

- **Have you ever been so mad about how you were treated in a group that you considered quitting? How did you work through your issue with the group?**
- **How would you feel if you were ignored by your friends?**

However, Leilani didn't want to let anyone down at the meet. In the locker room before the meet, she tried to calm her angry nerves with breathing exercises and stretches, just as their coach had taught them. That's when she heard someone crying. Around an island of lockers, she found Izzy, her team's best diver, sitting on a bench with her head in her hands. Even though Izzy had been one of the girls whispering about her, Leilani was still concerned that she was crying.

"Hey, what's up, Izzy?" Leilani asked. "Why haven't you put your suit on yet?"

"What's the point?" Izzy asked. "I'm not diving today."

Leilani frowned. "Wait. What?"

"I had period cramps during last week's tryouts for the meet," Izzy said, rolling her eyes. "So I didn't dive my best and blew it big time. Coach is putting in Marisol instead of me."

Leilani shook her head. "I don't understand. Marisol is a great swimmer, but she's not as good of a diver as you are."

TALK ABOUT IT

- **Why might Leilani be worried about Izzy even though she's also angry with her?**
- **How could Leilani have acted more like a leader before and during her conversation with Izzy?**

"According to the coach's new rule, she is," Izzy grumbled. "We all have to live with it. Well, except you of course."

Leilani felt a momentary pang of guilt, but her defensive instincts quickly took over. "This isn't my fault."

"I'm not saying it is," Izzy snapped. "I just want to dive."

Leilani sighed. "What am I supposed to do about it, Izzy? I didn't make the new policy—the coach did. Sorry I won too many meets and you're jealous that I'm the captain."

"Geez, relax," said Izzy. "This isn't about you at all. None of us are *jealous* of you. We're upset that you're not sticking up for the rest of your team because of this unfair policy." She looked at Leilani expectantly.

Leilani wanted to react in anger again, but she took a deep breath and closed her eyes. Anger wouldn't solve anything, and she needed to really listen to what Izzy was saying—especially if it was impacting the whole team. "I'm sorry, I'm just as upset as you are about the whole thing," Leilani said. "But that's the way it is. What can I possibly do?"

TALK ABOUT IT

- **Have you ever thought a situation revolved around you but then realized that it affected others too? What did you do?**
- **What leadership qualities does Leilani display when she talks to Izzy?**

Izzy looked down. "Maybe you could try talking to the coach about the new policy? Some of us have tried without any success, but she might listen to you since you're the captain."

"I don't think I can change anything for this meet," Leilani said, "but I'll talk to Coach Keahi afterward about the policy. It's not fair that you don't get to participate at all."

"It's not fair that you don't get to participate at all."

Izzy smiled for the first time that Leilani could remember all week. "I'm sorry about snapping at you, you know," Izzy said.

"I was just frustrated, but that wasn't fair of me to do. It's not your fault either."

"I'm going to try my best to fix this," Leilani replied.

Leilani was still disheartened with the team's morale by the time for her last event, the 100-meter butterfly. Normally, the butterfly was her best event. But she just didn't have the heart to continue, especially since the team had performed poorly overall during the entire meet. No matter how hard the swimmers and divers tried, they couldn't break the top three. Leilani swam as hard as she could, but her heart wasn't in it. She came in sixth, her worst placement the entire season. After the meet, when

everyone was changing back into their clothes to get on the bus, Coach Keahi pulled Leilani over to the side of the locker room.

"What happened out there?" she asked, frowning. "Everyone seemed to lack the wind in their sails."

Leilani was nervous to stand up to Coach Keahi, but she didn't want to let her team down again. She had to rally on behalf of her friends, no matter what. "The girls are really upset about the new rule about tryouts before the meets," Leilani said. "While I know you wanted it to be fairer and give everyone a shot, it ended up making things difficult for the team. I mean, Izzy didn't even get to swim or dive at all today."

Coach Keahi flipped her papers over on her clipboard. "Of course Izzy swam today! She did the—oh, you're right," Coach Keahi said. "Goodness, I didn't even realize that she wouldn't participate today."

Leilani said, "Yeah, I know it really upset her. And the rest of the team isn't happy either. Could we meet after school to discuss it?"

"Of course," Coach Keahi said. "Thank you for talking with me about it. We can go over some other ways to make the meet events fair."

For the first time since she'd been named team captain, Leilani didn't feel angry. She felt encouraged by her coach's positive response. Maybe Leilani could turn this around and be a better leader after all.

ASK THE EXPERT

In order to be a more effective leader, Leilani needed to lead with humility. Humility is the understanding that you're not the center of everything, a trait that can go a long way toward building trust in a group. At the same time, believing in yourself is essential for excelling at any skill, just as it's important for being a leader. The balance between believing in yourself and being humble can be difficult for many leaders to achieve.

Sometimes it can be difficult to understand that the needs and feelings of others are as important and valid as yours. Leaders lacking in humility run the risk of alienating the people in their group by underestimating or ignoring the needs of others. Leilani was an ineffective captain until she started to figure out how to get everyone's emotions in check, including her own.

While being aware of your own emotional response and validating the emotions of others is a first step to improving emotions in your group, you should expect it to be a continuous process of growing. Once your group sees you making the effort to learn what's causing their resentment, and they can tell that you're taking steps to correct the situation, it's more likely your group will grow to trust you.

GET HEALTHY

- Write a short script in which one person is upset about being treated unfairly but the other person sees only his or her own point of view. How is the conflict resolved in your script?
- Find an article in your local news about someone who led with humility. How did that person lead the group? Did the leader's followers work to accomplish the leader's goals?
- Think about someone who you think was a good leader of a group you belonged to. What did you like about that leadership style? Which skills did that person use to lead successfully?

THE LAST WORD FROM ANNE

We often look to leaders for inspiration and support. While that's a big part of a leader's job, it's impossible for a leader to be strong all the time. But a person who wants to lead will sometimes need to take a close look at what she's feeling and put it in perspective. The ability to understand and control your emotions is called self-management, and developing this skill will help you make better decisions as a leader.

A willingness to listen to the needs of others is essential to being a humble leader, since it demonstrates that you value the opinions and feelings of people other than yourself. I've definitely known people like Leilani, who were so focused with their own problems that they didn't see what was happening in front of them. Unfortunately, some people resist learning to be humble because their ego gets in the way. Sometimes it takes words from an honest, outspoken friend to make people see reality.

CHAPTER FIVE

NO MORE HOMEWORK EVER!

Leaders naturally want to be compelling and charismatic so that people will want to follow them, but sometimes their urge to please everyone can get them into trouble and even cause harm. Say you promise potential followers that if they allow you to be leader, you'll make some change that will benefit them. That in itself is a normal exchange, because a leader's job is often to bring about improvements in a group or society. However, you need to be able to deliver on what you've offered.

Beware of making impossible promises such as a simple solutions to complex problems, something that will cost more money than you can raise, or anything that requires resources or control you don't have. In other words, be sure your promises are based in reality. If you don't, you'll end up with followers who've lost faith in you. That, in turn, may lead to a loss of your leadership position.

JUANA'S STORY

"Vote for Juana to get your free time back!" The signs were lettered in purple marker on big yellow sheets of poster board. One week before the election for tenth-grade class president, Juana taped them up in every hallway.

"What do you mean by that?" Michael asked Juana on Monday after biology, tapping on one of her signs. "How can you get our free time back?"

Although Juana longed for a chance to tell people her big promise, it was essential that she not let any of the teachers hear her. They would try to stop her from campaigning. Once she was in office, they'd have to deal with the change. Until then, it was better to keep what she envisioned under wraps. "I mean no more homework," she said softly.

Once she was in office, they'd have to deal with the change.

Michael's eyes opened wide. "Like, ever?"

"Not for the rest of the year," Juana said with a smile.

"Oh, wow. That would be amazing," Michael said. "How are you going to do that?"

Juana mouthed a name. "Principal Morales."

Michael raised his eyebrows. "Wow. She's on board with this? Cool!"

In fact, Juana had a strong suspicion that Principal Morales would laugh her right out of her office if she asked for homework to be stopped. But Juana's strategy was to convince voters that she had an "in" with the principal until the principal didn't have a choice but to honor her demands.

The more classmates Juana talked to, the more her promise was whispered, texted, and tweeted. While walking through the halls and lunchroom, Juana heard her classmates gossiping about her and saw them point at her. This was her plan, to earn their attention by proving her commitment to every student's dream. If she could quietly convince everyone that homework would be history, she had a chance to be class president.

Her opponent Lien had zero personality, as far as Juana was concerned. Lien's signs were cool and even used QR codes that went to a campaign website, but she barely interacted with other students in their grade. And instead of coming up with a fun policy like Juana's, Lien had written an article for the school newspaper about wanting to improve the school's curriculum on climate change.

"If you vote for Lien," Juana joked to her classmates, "your homework will probably double."

***

The day before the election, both Juana and Lien participated in a debate in the gym. Mr. Robinson, the government teacher, was the moderator. From a chair facing the candidates, Mr. Robinson said, "Please state your platform. Lien, you may go first."

Lien used notecards and discussed her ideas for an elective course about climate

TALK ABOUT IT

- **What do you think of Lien's ideas? Would they help the school?**
- **Why do you think the students aren't interested in Lien's campaign?**

change, mandatory volunteer hours to help students who wanted to get into top colleges, and peer tutoring services in the math building before school. Everything she talked about sounded like work, work, work.

When it was her turn, Juana didn't give a speech, choosing instead to shout, "Who wants their free time back?"

"We do!" everyone called.

"Can you go into more detail?" asked Mr. Robinson. "Exactly how will you save your classmates time?"

"Just trust me," Juana said, trying to make eye contact with every single student. "I have a plan." The students nodded along, and Juana knew she had their votes.

The next morning, Juana cast a vote for herself. She was encouraged by the fact that, all day long, her classmates told her about their votes. "So, you'd better do what you promised," many of them added, some of them sounding less than friendly about it.

Juana started to worry what she'd do if Principal Morales didn't agree, leaving her unable to deliver. But she blocked out her concern, convincing herself that once she won, she only

She was encouraged by the fact that, all day long, her classmates told her about their votes.

had to ask Principal Morales to cancel all homework. And while Principal Morales would probably say no, what mattered was that Juana could say she tried, so no one could blame her.

***

The election results were given during announcements the next day. “And, by a landslide, the class president is Juana!” While the sound of joyful whooping erupted all over the school, Lien came over to Juana’s desk and shook her hand solemnly.

That afternoon, Juana went to see the principal, but the meeting hardly went as planned. "Well, congratulations, Juana," said Principal Morales. "Your classmates seem to believe in your message. But, it's too bad you're not going to be able to keep your campaign promises and cancel homework."

Juana gasped. "How did you know that's what I was going to ask?"

"It's my job to know what all the students are talking about," Principal Morales said. She folded her hands on her desk. "I'm disappointed in the way you ran your campaign, Juana. Many of the students thought I'd already agreed to suspend homework for the rest of the year."

Juana shifted in her seat. She felt uncomfortable. "I figured you would say no," Juana mumbled, "but that I could tell everyone I asked."

TALK ABOUT IT

- **Does a leader have an obligation to do what she promises, or is it OK to say things just to make people like you? Why or why not?**
- **How might Juana win back the trust of the student body?**

"Your classmates aren't going to be happy that you lied to them," the principal said. "You'll need to get them back on your side if you want to be successful in student government. What are your thoughts on how to do that?"

Juana's face felt hot. "I could apologize?"

"And what else?"

"And I could come up with a promise I can actually keep?"

"Now *that* sounds like a plan I can get behind," Principal Morales said. She smiled. "So I expect you to be ready with a speech tomorrow."

"Yes, Principal Morales," Juana said, realizing she wouldn't be getting much sleep that night.

But the next morning Juana showed up feeling invigorated by the challenge of writing a believable apology and a practical promise. Since there hadn't been time to arrange another assembly, Principal Morales asked Juana to make her remarks during morning announcements.

Her speech was short, and though Juana was nervous about how her classmates would react, she knew that she had to be truthful. She ended her speech by saying, "I am sorry for promising something that I knew probably wouldn't happen. However, I intend to make good on my promises to discuss the overwhelming amount of homework we receive each week in our classes. While I don't know what the outcome will be yet, I'm going to meet with representatives from the faculty to discuss the homework load and see what we can do to fix it." She looked straight into the camera and added, "You have my word."

TALK ABOUT IT

- **Is Juana the only one who learned a valuable lesson, or do you think those who voted for her did too? If so, what lesson did they learn?**
- **Do you think her new promise will appease her disappointed voters? What are some challenges that Juana might face in the future because of her broken campaign promises?**

ASK THE EXPERT

Although it's important for a leader to have a vision and inspire her followers, always be aware of what you're doing to gain power. It's common for followers to put someone in power just because they like her. But if you promise something unrealistic, you'll be forced to leave that debt unpaid and your followers disappointed and angry. The words associated with a leader are her responsibility, as are whatever actions or feelings result from them.

Like Juana, you may find that you've promised something you can't deliver. If that happens, the most important action is to own up to your mistake. As was true in Juana's case, that might mean scaling back or restructuring a promise so that it reflects reality.

No one expects you to be a magician. To be a good leader, you just need to do what's best for your group. Promising things that can't come true will distract from your group's actual goals. Besides, as tempting as it may seem to promise the impossible, that unattainable dream could end up ruining a whole organization.

GET HEALTHY

- Think of something you really wish you could change about your school or other community group. Is there a practical way to do it? Will people with authority approve the project? Is there a way to raise money for it?
- Imagine someone is trying to sway your opinion or get you to vote for something. Think about what would be effective and get your attention.
- Make a campaign poster for a position you'd like to have, be it in your school, your community, or even a national office. What are some realistic things you could promise your followers?

THE LAST WORD FROM ANNE

Maybe Juana truly wished she could stop teachers from giving homework, realizing how much her fellow students would love it. Wishing she could fulfill the promise, she went ahead with a plan that had no basis in reality. But the fact that she didn't intend to trick anyone doesn't make her actions OK. She was being the type of leader who doesn't have a realistic sense of what's possible. Hoping to make your wildest wishes come true isn't the approach of a responsible leader.

Even if your intention isn't to lie or mislead, people can get hurt if you offer them something you can't give them. Imagine a coach who promised to make your team win every game, ignoring the terrible record it's had for the past five seasons. That's not a promise someone could easily keep. If the leaders can't deliver, it's the followers who usually have to pay the price.

CHAPTER SIX

PEER PRESSURE

Leaders often find themselves in situations in which they witness behavior they know is wrong. However, sometimes calling out that behavior poses a risk. Maybe they'll lose friends or get someone in trouble, or maybe they'll make authority figures angry at them. Nevertheless, good leaders understand that staying silent isn't an option, so they do the right thing despite the personal consequences. A person who behaves ethically and honorably when confronted with a tough choice is a person who has what it takes to be a good leader.

That feeling inside that tells you what is right and wrong is sometimes called your moral center. If you pay attention to what your moral center is telling you, you'll make better decisions as a leader, even when it's far from easy. Jazlin learned this the hard way when she disagreed with her friends about how to treat others.

JAZLIN'S STORY

Jazlin, Rhiannon, and Sahar were constantly together. Besides walking to school as a trio, they also ate lunch at the same table and had neighboring desks in their classes. Sometimes their teachers separated them because they couldn't stop talking to each other, even for an hour.

Sahar was smart and outgoing, never running out of ideas for what they should do or talk about. Rhiannon did everything Sahar suggested without hesitating, which included buying similar clothes and wearing a similar hairstyle. She even laughed like crazy at all of Sahar's jokes.

Sometimes she looked around at the other kids in her classes and wondered whether she should make some more friends.

As for Jazlin, these friends were her life. Having known them since first grade, she couldn't picture her day without them. But sometimes she looked around at the other kids in her classes and wondered whether she should make some more friends. Because the process of befriending new people seemed like so much effort, she just stuck with the people she knew best. Rhiannon and Sahar were like family, not to mention that she feared making Sahar jealous if she found someone else to hang out with.

TALK ABOUT IT

- **Have you ever been in a group of friends where one person seemed like the leader? How did that affect the friendship?**
- **Why might Jazlin stick with her two oldest friends instead of branching out to meet new people?**

***

One afternoon when they were waiting for the bus home, a cute boy named Jack from their Earth science class was waiting nearby. Secretly, Jazlin thought Jack was kind of a jerk, but because she knew Sahar had a crush on him, she didn't say anything negative.

Suddenly Sahar hurried over to Jack. She appeared to shake his hand, which was a very odd thing to do. Even stranger was the fact that Jack didn't seem surprised by Sahar's actions, merely nodding his head and grinning. Hoping Rhiannon could explain what was happening, Jazlin turned to her, but Rhiannon only put her index finger in front of her mouth, as if she had the answer but wasn't about to share.

"What was that?" Jazlin demanded when Sahar slid back into the bus line.

"What was what?" Sahar asked innocently.

A strange feeling of numbness crept over Jazlin, since this was the first time she was aware of Sahar and Rhiannon pairing

up against her. Refusing to take her eyes off Jack, she watched him tuck a folded piece of cotton candy pink paper into his backpack. There was only one person in their grade who used that color paper, and it certainly wasn't Sahar, who never got tired of making fun of Carrie for using it. "Sahar, did you steal something from Carrie and give it to Jack?"

"Sahar, did you steal something from Carrie and give it to Jack?"

"What, no?" Sahar said, defensive. "And what business is it of yours if I did?"

Not knowing how to answer that, Jazlin climbed onto the bus. All the way home, Sahar whispered nonstop about how cute Jack was. When Sahar asked if Jazlin wanted to come over to her house after school, Jazlin shook her head. She wasn't sure how she felt about what she had seen and just wanted to go home.

"I have to study for the social studies test," Jazlin said. "Sorry, I'll see you tomorrow." Jazlin walked to the front of the bus without looking back.

That night, she couldn't get the incident out of her mind. She half-heartedly texted back while Sahar and Rhiannon gushed over Jack. But at the same time, she kept replaying Sahar's interaction with Jack involving the pink piece of paper.

***

When Jazlin arrived at school the next morning, she saw Carrie thumbing nervously at the pink notebook they always carried. Jazlin didn't really know Carrie, but they seemed very upset. "Everything OK?" Jazlin asked.

Carrie looked down and nodded hesitantly. "Yeah, I mean. Sure."

Jazlin frowned. "Did somebody take something from you?"

TALK ABOUT IT

- **Have you ever seen somebody you like do something you knew was wrong? What are some things you can do if that happens?**
- **What are some types of behavior so unethical that they would convince you to break up a friendship?**

Now Carrie looked up shyly and said, "My quiz study sheet that I made."

TALK ABOUT IT

- **Is there someone in your school who is often victimized or bullied? Have you ever stood by while that person was bullied? Why or why not?**
- **What are some ways you can make your school safer for people who are being bullied?**

The pieces of the puzzle were beginning to fit together. "Was it Sahar?" Jazlin asked, even though she was pretty sure she knew the answer. When Carrie nodded miserably, Jazlin said, "Wait here."

Jazlin took a few steps toward Sahar's locker, then stopped, wondering what she should say or even whether she should get involved. Glancing back at Carrie, who looked so destroyed and lost, Jazlin found the nerve to walk up to Sahar. Her jaw was tense as she spoke. "Did you take Carrie's notes?"

Sahar didn't even look at her. "What? Just because Carrie's a nerd, that doesn't mean I took their notes."

"Carrie said you took them."

"Then Carrie's a liar and you're a traitor," Sahar snapped. It was such a hostile response that Jazlin felt like she'd been slapped. She suddenly felt like she didn't even know this person she was supposed to be best friends with.

Quickly, Jazlin's shock turned to anger. "Get Carrie's notes back and I won't tell anyone about the awful thing you did," Jazlin demanded in a steady voice.

Now Sahar slammed her locker and glared at Jazlin. "Oh, please," Sahar said dramatically. "Carrie doesn't need their notes to pass the quiz, and Jack won't get above an F without them. And Jack said he'd take me to a movie this weekend if I snagged Carrie's study guide for him."

For a few seconds, Jazlin could hardly breathe. She was disappointed and stunned by Sahar's behavior. Part of her was worried that she was about to lose a friend, but Jazlin knew she had to do what was right even if it would make Sahar mad. "If you don't return that study guide before first period," Sahar said, "I'm going to tell Ms. Weller that you and Jack are planning to cheat on the quiz."

Jazlin knew she had to do what was right even if it would make Sahar mad.

Sahar looked furious. "You wouldn't dare."

Slightly more confident, Jazlin said, "I absolutely would."

Apparently Sahar knew she wasn't bluffing, because she immediately turned and walked off. Jazlin followed to make sure she'd actually stick to her word. Jack was upset, but when

Sahar whispered something in his ear, he glanced at Jazlin and frowned, looking nervous. When he gave the paper back to Sahar, Sahar marched over to Jazlin and pushed the piece of paper into the middle of her chest. Jazlin hoped Sahar might apologize, but Sahar turned and walked away, Rhiannon following close behind. Even though her stomach dropped thinking about losing her best friends, Jazlin knew she'd done the right thing. And the way Carrie smiled when Jazlin returned their study sheet only proved it.

TALK ABOUT IT

- **Do you think there's anything Jazlin could have done or said to prevent this situation from unfolding? How might she have stood up for Carrie sooner?**
- **Do you think a lifelong friendship is worth trying to preserve no matter what? Should Jazlin reach out to Sahar and try to patch things up? Why or why not?**

ASK THE EXPERT

The word *ethics* means a code of right and wrong, and strong ethics is an essential element for a strong leader. While not everything you face in life will fit neatly into that code, it can serve you well as a starting point to guide you through tough decisions such as the one Jazlin faced. She realized she'd probably lose her friendship with Sahar and Rhiannon if she stood up for Carrie. However, she decided that cheating and stealing was so wrong that it was worth that risk to stand up against her friends.

Sahar was willing to act cruelly just to get what she wanted. Her goal was for Jack to go out with her, and acting unethically was an acceptable price to pay. Those aren't the actions of a successful leader.

Moral decision-making refers to a willingness to do what you know to be right even if it's an unpopular point of view or will cause unwelcome disruption in your life. That kind of decision is often required of leaders, but if you rely on your sense of ethics, it can guide you through moments like the one Jazlin faced.

GET **HEALTHY**

- Journal about a time that you did—or considered doing—something you felt was wrong, just because everyone else was doing it. How did it make you feel? Now write down a list of ways that you could avoid doing something like that again.
- Think of something that's happening in your community that you feel sure is wrong. Write a speech you could give to inspire your community to stand up against this situation.
- Surround yourself with friends and peers who aren't bullies. If someone is taking advantage of another student, stand up for what you know is right.

THE LAST WORD FROM **ANNE**

Jazlin turned into a leader at a crucial moment when someone needed her help. Although the loss of Sahar's friendship wasn't what she expected, let alone wanted, that seemed the only possible right action to her.

Jazlin helped a classmate at the significant personal cost of losing her two oldest friends. Her moral center was so strong that it wouldn't let her live with the injustice she witnessed, meaning that she *had* to do something. And by standing up to a bully and reaching out to a victim, she showed others how to behave. That's real leadership.

CHAPTER SEVEN

A GENTLE APPROACH

Some leaders are comfortable taking the lead, stepping in with so much confidence that they act as a natural source of inspiration to their followers. On the other hand, some leaders don't believe in themselves, causing them to worry that they don't belong out in front. Such a leader might fear that nobody will want to follow her, which in turn may push her to try too hard, feeling desperate to convince everyone else that she's in charge. There are also leaders who assume they're better and smarter than everyone else, believing they're superior with an automatic privilege to fill that role.

A leader with low self-confidence might speak in a condescending way to others to make herself feel more powerful. She may feel the urge to prove she's in control of every aspect of the group by criticizing and complaining about everything her followers do. Conversely, if a leader is convinced she's superior to everyone else, she might rely on negative emotions such as fear and hate or negative actions such as handing out punishments.

Treating people this way isn't good leadership—it's bullying. Becoming an effective leader means approaching any situation with both confidence in your leadership abilities as well as the humility to understand that you might not be correct 100 percent of the time. A gentler approach that involves guiding your followers rather than demanding something from them often raises the spirits of everyone in the group, rather than tearing them down.

MIRIAM'S STORY

"I told you we needed ten boxes of large black trash bags," Miriam said loudly to Aaron, one of her volunteers for Parks Clean-Up Weekend. He was younger than Miriam and flinched when she yelled because the park was otherwise quiet. "The town council said *I* was in charge, so you need to do what I say."

Aaron looked at the ground and shook his head. "I could only get eight boxes. You didn't give me enough money for ten, and my mom said we couldn't afford to buy any ourselves."

TALK ABOUT IT

- **How do you think Aaron felt after being spoken to like that?**
- **If Miriam had really listened to what Aaron was trying to say, what do you think she would have learned?**

"Then you should have figured out something else!" Miriam said. "You could have gone to a different store where they're cheaper. If you're going to work on this committee, you have to really do your part." Miriam walked away before Aaron could come up with any more excuses.

"If you're going to work on this committee, you have to really do your part."

On a bench a few yards away sat a couple of girls from one of the three schools participating in the clean-up. Miriam glared at them and shook her head, wishing it were just students from her own school so she didn't have to deal with strangers. They were laughing and joking around, looking at something on their phones, when they clearly should have been working. One girl took a selfie of the two of them on the bench. Miriam was furious. She marched over to them.

"If you don't know how to do your job, I'll find someone else who does. Now, what are you supposed to be doing?" She swiped

her finger over her tablet screen, scrolling through a list. "What are your names again?"

"Hi!" said the girl who had taken the selfie. "I'm Lea, and this is my friend Erika. We're from Northfield High."

"If you don't know how to do your job, I'll find someone else who does."

Miriam looked down quickly and didn't return Lea's smile. "OK, here you are. You were supposed to be putting up signs that show the workers where to go. Think you can handle that? It could've been finished by now."

Lea gave Miriam a funny look, then said, "It *is* finished. We did it just like you asked." She pointed out six different spots around the park, each marked with a red sign on a wooden post. "One numbered sign for each work area, hammered eight inches into the grass, exactly like you said. Did you need us to do something else?"

"What? No. OK." Embarrassed, Miriam turned

TALK ABOUT IT

- **How much of Miriam's behavior toward Lea and Erika was because they came from a different school? Why might this be a factor?**
- **What kind of impression do you think Miriam made on those two girls by not thanking them for putting up the signs?**

quickly and walked away. Miriam's jaw clenched. Those Northfield girls seemed like jerks.

Across the picnic lawn, she recognized two students from her own school, Amber and Shane. They were struggling to put up a canopy. The plan was to set up the registration table under it, but a strong breeze had caught one side of the nylon fabric, making it bulge as they stretched it out.

"What are you *doing*?" Miriam had already started shouting when she was only halfway across the grass. "Your guideline is too loose, Amber. Are you trying to make the canopy blow away?"

Amber gave her a goofy grin. "Sorry to be a klutz. I've never done this before."

"Well, it doesn't take a genius put one of these together."

As the smile left Amber's face, Shane spoke up. "Why are you being so mean, Miriam?"

"It's my responsibility to make sure everything gets done. And here you two are, messing this up. What do you want me to say?"

"We're figuring it out," Shane retorted. "Just give us a few minutes."

Amber grabbed frantically at the canopy's corner trying

TALK ABOUT IT

- **Have you ever been made fun of for not doing a task well that you found very difficult? How did that make you feel?**
- **What is Shane's role in this story? Does he have a particular effect on Miriam's understanding of the situation? How might Miriam have interacted differently with Shane if she'd talked to him first?**

to fix it. Miriam shook her head and then asked, "Do you want a different partner, Shane? Someone who knows what they're doing?"

"I said I was sorry," Amber said in a shaky voice. Her chin quivered as she dropped the canopy and hunched her shoulders.

Shane gave Amber a big hug and then turned fiercely to Miriam. "We were doing fine until you came along. What's your problem?"

"I'm trying to lead," Miriam snapped.

"Well you're not doing a very good job," Shane replied, turning his back to Miriam so he could comfort Amber.

Feeling furious at everyone and everything, Miriam strode to the edge of park and sat down to think. She didn't know how everything could go so incredibly wrong or why she felt like such a failure as a leader. Slowly she let her gaze wander from Shane and Amber huddling together under the half-raised canopy, to the girls from Northfield High whispering and pointing at her, to shy little Aaron kicking a stack of garbage bags.

She didn't know how everything could go so incredibly wrong or why she felt like such a failure as a leader.

They all looked so miserable, and it was because she had made them feel that way. Miriam was trying to lead, but in the process she realized that she'd just been mean.

After sitting for a few more minutes to pull herself together, Miriam walked back to Aaron's station and said, "I'm sorry for getting mad earlier. We can make it work with eight boxes of garbage bags, and if we need more, I'll just pop over to the store and get them." The look of relief on his face made Miriam feel ashamed of her earlier behavior.

Her next stop was the girls from Northfield, who were still sitting on the bench. "Hey, Lea and Erika, I just wanted to say that the signs look great. And also, thank you for volunteering today." The hostility left the girls' faces, and they smiled.

Hardest of all was making herself talk to Amber and Shane. Miriam realized she'd been unfair to them, especially Amber, and she also knew she had to apologize. "I'm so sorry I spoke to you that way," she admitted, "but I've never been put in charge of anything this big before, and I guess I'm just really stressed that things won't be perfect. Is there anything I can do to make it up to you?"

"We sure could use a hand putting up this canopy," said Amber.

"You got it," said Miriam. She was determined to be a better leader from then on.

ASK THE EXPERT

Miriam clearly had some issues to work through before she could be a good leader. At first, she didn't give the members of her group enough credit, which made them feel unappreciated and resentful. But Miriam also lacked empathy for her followers, especially Aaron and Amber, both of whom were doing their best under the circumstances.

Miriam didn't listen to Aaron, and she ignored Amber's willingness to help in favor of correcting her. Shane's reply that Miriam was a bad leader was quite accurate. Some leaders believe that doling out harsh words makes them stronger. While it's true that speaking cruelly to someone can cause them to shrink and seem less powerful than you, it does nothing to increase your own value as a leader or as a person in general.

Miriam feared that she wouldn't be a good leader, yet that very fear contributed to her being a poor leader. As soon as she started to correct her errors by apologizing, demonstrating patience, and thanking people, everyone's attitude seemed to lift.

GET **HEALTHY**

- Think of someone who's done something positive in your life. Write them a text or give them a call to thank them.
- If there is somebody who has not done what you consider an ideal job at some task, find a time to speak to them constructively so they can do a better job in the future, but don't make them feel bad about what you think they did wrong.
- If you see somebody not get the thanks they deserve, be the one who thanks them.
- The next time you see a leader speaking harshly to somebody who didn't do things exactly right, speak to that leader privately.

THE LAST WORD FROM **ANNE**

Criticism is powerful but often misunderstood. It doesn't have to be a bad thing, and it doesn't have to be a power play to make somebody feel small. It can be a conversation, particularly when you use constructive criticism that encourages the person you're talking with to grow and improve. If you think someone could do a task differently or more efficiently, it makes sense to discuss your reasoning and come up with a solution for how it could be done better in the future. If the person did some parts of the task well, mention those too. That's a lot more helpful than barking complaints at somebody, since talking only about what you don't like will just make people feel bad.

A good leader knows how to build up her group as she leads. People who feel good about themselves are more likely to succeed and feel motivated to help the group meet its goals. There is no upside to tearing people down.

CHAPTER EIGHT

HELP WANTED

Even if you can name every character and describe every episode of your favorite TV show, could you make the show yourself if someone handed you a camera and said, "Film the next season"? It's likely you wouldn't even know where to begin. That's what experts are for. Nobody knows how to do everything, and that's OK.

Trying something new or ambitious is a great way to stretch yourself while you discover your capabilities and talents. But you can't be expected to become an expert on everything. The key to being a good leader is finding someone who knows what you don't and listening to their expertise. You'll get to meet new people as you develop another important leadership skill—convincing others to get involved in your project. And you never know—the people you meet in one project might be the perfect connections for another project down the road.

Sometimes it's necessary to lead a group in doing something that's outside your zone of comfort and knowledge. But there's no reason to face the challenge alone. If you look hard enough, you'll find people who know how to do it. If you reach out to them in a respectful and effective way, you're likely to find some who are glad to help. Hannah found this out when she took on a larger project than she could handle alone.

HANNAH'S STORY

Hannah had loved going to the theater since she'd seen her first children's show when she was six. Now that she was in high school, she attended plays staged by the community theater group. Rather than feeling any ambition to be a performer, she really enjoyed thinking about what went on behind the scenes.

One day at dinner, Hannah's mom told her that Red Pines Home for Seniors, where she worked, was seriously lacking in entertainment for the residents. "I sure wish we could find some volunteers, like maybe some musicians or something. There must be someone out there who would perform for the elderly."

Hannah thought about this all evening until just before she got into bed, she suddenly had an idea so brilliant that she had to run downstairs. "I've got it!" she announced. "I'll put on a play for them."

Her mom seemed doubtful. "That's a huge responsibility."

Hannah was a little offended, considering how organized she was and how much she loved theater. She presented her strategy to defend her enthusiasm. "I'll find a play, get some costumes, and hold auditions. Right?" A little bit of doubt crept into her heart, which she tried to ignore. "Oh, and I can look in the thrift shop and on eBay for props."

"That's a lot of 'I,'" said her mom. "Nobody puts on a play by herself."

Hannah pictured the backstage tour she once went on at the community theater, where she'd seen a couple dozen

"Why don't you delegate some of the responsibility?"

people backstage, doing all sorts of jobs. "You're right," she admitted. "So, I guess I can't do it. Never mind."

"You're giving up already?" her mom asked with a laugh. "Why don't you delegate some of the responsibility?"

Hannah's mood brightened immediately. "Maybe I could convince a bunch of kids from school to pitch in and help."

With permission from the principal, Hannah put a notice in the school newsletter announcing a meeting for anyone interested in putting on a play. She checked out a copy of the play *Arsenic and Old Lace* from the library, a hilarious play the community theater had done two years before.

The night of the first meeting at school, she was prepared with notes on her phone to help her address the group. She'd brought tortilla chips and sparkling water, plus paper bowls, napkins, and cups. Soon kids both familiar and new to her started to file in, sitting in the desks and looking at her expectantly.

TALK ABOUT IT

- **Why do you think some people have trouble delegating tasks? How might they improve that skill?**
- **Have you ever taken on too much? If so, how did you handle it? If not, what might you do to make things split more evenly?**

As she started speaking, Hannah's hands shook so much that she almost dropped her phone. "Hi. I'm Hannah. I'm hoping you'll all help me put on a play." She told them about the senior home and described the plot of *Arsenic and Old Lace* before asking whether anyone had questions. Six hands shot up. The questions weren't what she expected.

Six hands shot up. The questions weren't what she expected.

"Are we going to have a lighting designer?"

"Will our stage be proscenium or theater-in-the-round?"

"Is there a sound system, and do we have access to body mics?"

"What's our budget?"

"How many rehearsals will we have per week?"

"Who's going to direct the play?"

Hannah didn't know the answer to a single one of those questions, but she tried to assure the attendees that everything would be worked out in time. The meeting continued with kids shouting out suggestions and Hannah typing all of them into her phone. She had no idea what was possible and what wasn't. But at least she got the group to agree to meet two afternoons a week.

Hannah delegated a few tasks that came up right away, putting two students in charge of finding out what the space in the senior home was like and another in charge of costume ideas. Someone else said he wanted to figure out how to do sets with nothing but free and donated items, so she encouraged him to do so.

TALK ABOUT IT

- **Does the fact that Hannah can't answer the group's questions mean that she isn't a good leader? Why or why not?**
- **Is there something else Hannah could have done to prepare for this meeting? What other things could she have considered before holding a meeting?**

But there were still so many questions racing through Hannah's mind on her walk home. It seemed unrealistic to learn every single thing about running a show. By the time she reached her house, she was ready to give up. "I'm not qualified to do this," she complained to her mom, slamming the door behind her. "I don't know how to put on a play. There's too much to consider."

"I don't know how to put on a play. There's too much to consider."

Her mom just smiled, which made Hannah more furious.

"What?" Hannah demanded.

"Can you think of any people in our area who know about theater?"

Puzzling over this, Hannah said, "Well, the community theater obviously has directors and people who know about stage lights and stuff."

Her mom said, "Maybe you could ask for their help."

"But I was going to lead this project," Hannah argued. "I wanted to put on the play with other students, not have a bunch of professionals do it."

TALK ABOUT IT

- **What could Hannah say to convince the theater to help her?**
- **Have you ever approached a professional to give you advice or help with a project? If so, what did you ask? How was it received? If you haven't, what would you say when asking for help?**

"Your job is to make sure everything gets done right," her mom pointed out. "That includes finding people who can help you do it."

Hannah pictured senior citizens at the home, clapping and laughing in the audience of her play. She had to remember that this wasn't about her—it was about making the play the best it could be. "You're right. I'll email the community theater in the morning and ask if they can help."

Her email earned a quick, positive response from the theater's house manager, who invited Hannah to attend one of their rehearsals and speak to the director afterward. The minute she walked into that theater, she noticed how terrific the sets looked and how everyone on the crew seemed like they knew exactly what they were doing. There was no doubt in her mind that going to professionals for advice was the best decision she could have made.

ASK THE EXPERT

Hannah resisted the idea of asking for expert help because she was worried that she wouldn't be the leader anymore. Her mom then reminded her that asking for help is in itself a sign of leadership. Asking for help is useful on all types of projects, from a volunteer community effort to a big corporation trying something new. Bringing in experts from outside your group can turn a failing project into something not just successful but very special.

One noteworthy leadership skill is networking. Networking is the process of building social connections that may help you later in your career or other projects. It's especially important for leaders who might need to convince well-qualified experts to help with their projects.

It's great to be willing to listen to advice so you can avoid as many mistakes as possible. But things are going to go wrong at some point. If you can see your mistakes as part of the learning process, you'll get much more out of a project. And you can do an even better job next time!

GET **HEALTHY**

- Draft a polite email or letter you could send to a professional in a field that interests you. How might you ask that person for help? What ways do you think they could provide help?
- Imagine some big project you'd like to make a reality in your community. List five specific tasks that you don't know how to do yourself. Then list five experts who could help you with those tasks.
- When someone asks you if they can help you with something, is your response usually a defensive "No, I can handle it"? Next time, let them help you. Maybe it will make the project easier and better.

THE LAST WORD FROM **ANNE**

Being a leader doesn't mean you need total control at all times. The role of a successful leader normally changes as a project goes on, so sometimes you'll be the leader and sometimes you'll follow the directions of an expert. Don't be afraid to let other people who know more than you take the lead for their part of a job. That's the whole reason to have them around, and your project will be better for it.

Delegating is another skill Hannah had to apply to her project because there were too many tasks for her to execute or oversee. If you can find people who are interested in a particular aspect of a project, it can only make the project better when you let them help. And those people will also be happier members of your group because they've been invited to participate.

A SECOND LOOK

Maybe you've heard of the Swedish activist Greta Thunberg. In 2018, when she was 15, Greta sat down all alone in front of the Parliament building in the capital city of Stockholm. She held a sign that said "School Strike for Climate" in Swedish, hoping the government would notice her and act against climate change. By 2019, she was leading a worldwide Climate Strike day, having inspired millions of her peers to march in the streets to save the planet.

Many people looked at Greta and assumed that she would not be a great leader because she was a quiet young girl. However, Greta found a cause she was passionate about. She gathered information, talked to experts, and acted on her principles. Most of all, she found the courage to act and inspire others to change. She made a choice and took a risk with no way to predict whether it would have any real impact.

Since there's no way to know exactly what will happen when we make a choice, it's important to be brave enough to try anyway. But even if you don't want to lead on a global scale and inspire a whole generation, you can still find meaningful ways to lead. Remember Mia, who rallied her friends into joining her at the animal rescue? She let her passion for animals drive her natural leadership instincts, inspiring a few people to do important work. And don't forget the soccer captain, Wei, who led her team out of group-wide discord by listening actively to her teammates. Or Miriam, whose angst over her leadership responsibilities caused her to treat others poorly until she had the courage to assess the situation and apologize.

With so many opportunities to step up in life, you just might find that you're a great leader after all. You'll never know until you try.

YOUR FRIEND,
ANNE

PAY IT FORWARD

Being a leader does not look like one specific thing. In fact, you may already have some of the leadership qualities mentioned in this book without even knowing it! Now that you know what to focus on, you can pay it forward to a friend too. Remember the Get Healthy tips throughout this book, then take these steps to get healthy and get going.

1. Practice active listening so you truly understand what people are saying to you. Remember that active listening means that you're not constantly waiting for the moment when it's your turn to speak.

2. Don't pass up an opportunity to try new activities or meet new people. You never know what skills you'll learn or what connections you'll make.

3. When you're leading a project, try to see it from the point of view of the people in your group. If you have assigned tasks to people, are those tasks practical, or are they simply things you don't want to do?

4. Be patient and clear with people who are afraid of change. Your job as a leader is to explain clearly and patiently both why

your new idea will be an improvement and why the work of learning unfamiliar processes will be worth it in the long run.

5. Don't let negative emotions push you to speak disrespectfully. There's a big difference between discussing two sides of an argument and throwing insults at people.

6. Lead something you're passionate about. When people see how much you love something and how committed you are, they're more likely to follow your lead.

7. Use your sense of right and wrong to guide your actions, no matter what. If a situation feels wrong, it's probably wise to trust your instincts.

8. Learn from your mistakes, and don't let them stop your progress. Mistakes you make in how you handle problems, talk to people, or tackle a project can end up being incredibly valuable lessons for the next time you face something similar.

9. Try to think of leadership as a team effort. As you embark on new projects, seek out and welcome the skills that everyone has to offer so that the experience can be a true collaboration.

GLOSSARY

active listening

Listening with full concentration, trying hard to understand the speaker's point of view.

charismatic

Having charm that inspires devotion in others.

constructive criticism

Pointing out respectfully what you think could be better about something and why.

curriculum

The plan or course of study in a school; a plan for what lessons and information will be taught and how students will learn them.

delegate

To assign responsibility for various tasks to other people, usually within your work group.

ethics

Rules of behavior based on ideas about what is morally good and bad.

expertise
Advanced knowledge in a particular subject or field.

gossip
To talk about other people, typically including personal information or rumors.

humility
The quality or state of not thinking you are better than other people; a state of being humble.

resentment
The feeling that you were not treated fairly.

trait
A quality that defines a person's character, personality, or physical appearance.

youth group
A group of young people who gather for religious study.

ADDITIONAL

RESOURCES

SELECTED BIBLIOGRAPHY

Graham, Stedman. *Identity Leadership: To Lead Others You Must First Lead Yourself*. Center Street, 2019.

Kottler, Jeffrey A. *What You Don't Know about Leadership, But Probably Should: Applications to Daily Life*. Oxford UP, 2018.

Tan, Sherylle J., and Lisa DeFrank-Cole, editors. *Women's Leadership Journeys: Stories, Research, and Novel Perspectives*. Routledge, 2019.

FURTHER READINGS

Harris, Duchess, and Nancy Redd. *Growing Up a Girl*. Abdo, 2018.

Johnson, Maureen, editor. *How I Resist: Activism and Hope for a New Generation*. Wednesday, 2018.

Rich, KaeLyn. *Girls Resist! A Guide to Activism, Leadership, and Starting a Revolution*. Quirk, 2018.

ONLINE RESOURCES

To learn more about being a leader, please visit **abdobooklinks.com** or scan this QR code. These links are routinely monitored and updated to provide the most current information available.

MORE INFORMATION

For more information on this subject, contact or visit the following organizations:

Girls for a Change

100 Buford Rd.
North Chesterfield, VA 23235
girlsforachange.org

Girls for a Change is a nonprofit organization encouraging girls of color to visualize their bright futures and potential.

National Teen Leadership Program

PO Box 6278
Folsom, CA 95763-6278
ntlp.org

The National Teen Leadership Program (NTLP) runs camps and workshops in Sacramento, California, that teach teens leadership skills. Camp attendees come to these workshops from across the United States.

Teach a Girl to Lead

Center for American Women and Politics
Eagleton Institute of Politics
Rutgers, The State University of New Jersey
191 Ryders Ln.
New Brunswick, New Jersey 08901-8557
tag.rutgers.edu

Teach a Girl to Lead is a project created by the Center for American Women and Politics at Rutgers University. It provides resources and programs to help girls get involved in leadership opportunities across the United States.

INDEX

ABOUT THE AUTHOR

ANNE E. JOHNSON

Anne E. Johnson is a writer, musician, and teacher in New York City. She has published seven novels, nearly a hundred short stories, and several poems. Anne grew up in Wisconsin, where she discovered her favorite hobby: playing and singing Irish folk music. Now that she's in New York, she plays tunes on her fiddle and tin whistle and sings Irish ballads whenever she gets the chance.